EARTH'S HORIZONS
PANORAMA

Michèle Métail

translated by Marcella Durand

BSE

Earth's Horizons: Panorama by Michèle Métail
Translation © Marcella Durand, 2020

ISBN: 978-0-9997028-4-0

BSE Books are distributed by
  Small Press Distribution
  1341 Seventh Street
  Berkeley, CA 94710
  orders@spdbooks.org | www.spdbooks.org
  1-800-869-7553

BSE Books can also be purchased at
www.blacksquareeditions.org and www.hyperallergic.com

Contributions to BSE can be made to
  Off the Park Press, Inc.
  976 Kensington Ave.
  Plainfield, NJ 07060
  (Please make checks payable to Off the Park Press, Inc.)

To contact the Press please write:
  Black Square Editions
  1200 Broadway, Suite 3C
  New York, NY 10001

An independent subsidiary of Off the Park Press, Inc.
Member of CLMP.

Publisher: John Yau
Editors: Ronna Lebo and Boni Joi
Design & composition: Shanna Compton

Cover painting: Eve Aschheim, "LL-2" (2015), oil paint and graphite on
canvasboard, mounted, 16 x 12 inches. By permission of the artist.

A facsimile of the original French edition begins on page 39.

INTRODUCTION

Translation is in its nature literary, codifying and historicizing: it changes the potential energy of a work into kinetic language on a page, concrete, understood (somewhat), *read*. In a sense translation is a declaration of clarity, and even completion—in deciding that word means "this," and therefore, it means "this" enough to mean "this" in another language. Which is not at all what Michèle Métail's work is about. Instead, her work is anything but easily paraphrasable, reducible—or translatable. Its complexity takes shape in intricate constraints unique and integral to each work's origin and intent, and she often "publishes" as a performance that is as much auditory and visual experience as literary, using assonance, alliteration, varying vocal projections (including whispering) and image to create a holistic aesthetic experience. "The projection of words into space is the ultimate stage of writing, the affirmation of presence within language," she has written.[i] While she has now published over twenty books in France and other European countries, for many years she rejected traditional publication, searching instead to extend her work outward in ways deeply ephemeral, site specific, more engaged with how various genres such as music and film could carry poetry as well as paper. Toward these explorations, she cofounded Les Arts Contigus with her partner, composer

---

i *Métail to Durand via email, February 7, 2018.*

Louis Roquin, an association dedicated to the exploration of "genre transgression," which brings together dance, sculpture, installation, music and literature.

Perhaps Métail's best-known work in France is *Poème infini–Compléments de noms*, which is, as she describes it, "a single long modulation through a variety of languages and dialects."[ii] Begun in 1972 in Vienna, this "infinite poem" cycles nouns through a six-unit sentence structure: each added noun pushes the last out of the verse, not to be seen again. One translation by Tom La Farge:

> the captain of the company for excursions by steamboat on the Danube
>
> the wife of the captain of the company for excursions by steamboat
>
> the daughter of the wife of the captain of the company for excursions by boat
>
> the dog of the daughter of the wife of the captain of the company for excursions
>
> the kennel of the dog of the daughter of the wife of the captain of the company
>
> the carpet of the kennel of the dog of daughter of the wife of the captain
>
> the color of the carpet of the kennel of the dog of the daughter of the wife[iii]

The lines quoted above are part of a section of 2888 verses that correspond to the 2888 kilometers of the length of the Danube River (demonstrating how Métail's constraints are often site specific) and contain river/Danube-related content (also demonstrating how, for Métail, content is deeply related to form and constraint; one cannot exist without the other). Other manifestations

ii *Métail, bio, https://www.asymptotejournal.com/poetry/the-earths-horizons/*
iii *"Infinity, Minus Forty Yearly Installments: Noun Complements (1972-2012)," Michèle Métail, translated by Tom La Farge,* Words Without Borders, *December 2013.*

of *Poème infini* include radio performances and recordings played with dancers and musicians, writing verses on bank notes (according to Métail, an railroad employee read a verse out loud from one of the bank notes and then declared, "It doesn't mean anything"[iv]) and readings that were "unique and ephemeral"[v] to the location of the reading.

Métail credits *Poème infini* for her membership in Oulipo (Ouvroir de littérature potentielle)—she was one of the group's first female members, joining in 1975. However, she no longer associates closely with the group. While, according to membership rules, members may only resign by committing suicide in the presence of an officer of Oulipo and with the explicit intention to resign from Oulipo[vi], she has distanced herself from the group and its practices. In conversations with Métail, I understood that she is more interested in form and constraints as nonreproducible and unique to each piece—form is not so much an invention or "jeu" to be distributed further, but is instead organic to each piece's original intent and content. This commitment to form deeply bound to content might be better understood in context with her interest in Chinese poetry and in particular Chinese reversible poetry; in fact, Métail received her doctorate in ancient Chinese poetry. Her first book in English, *Wild Geese Returning: Chinese Reversible Poems*, was published by NYRB in 2017, and in it she discusses the fourth-century poet Su Shi (also known by her given name Su Hui) and her reversible poem, "Map of the Armillary Sphere," which she

---

iv *Ibid*

v *Ibid*

vi *Rule 9. (e) from "Introduction," Jacques Roubaud,* The Oulipo and Combinatorial Art, *reprinted in* Oulipo Compendium, *eds Harry Mathews and Alistair Brotchie, Atlas Press, 1998, pg. 38.*

embroidered on silk and sent to her husband after their estrangement. Here is how the empress of the Tang Dynasty, Wu Zetian, describes the work:

> "Mortified, Su Shi felt hatred and regret. Thus she embroidered the reversible poem. Five colors were intertwined; it was a treasure for the heart, a splendor for the eyes. This brocade measured eight inches long by eight inches wide, more than two hundred poems were inscribed there and one may count more than eight hundred words. Read vertically and horizontally, turned in one direction and then another, all ways offered poems."[vii]

The complex structure of this poem, analyzed in detail by Métail, is linked to cosmology, per the armillary sphere, which is an astronomical instrument, as well as to *The Book of Changes*; however, as Métail writes in her introduction to *Wild Geese Returning*, "revealing the structure of the poem still does not allow us to read it." But, perhaps even more powerfully, she writes, "Heaven, earth, and man entered into correspondences through the effect of numbers."

Numbers, as the basis of form, are thus the axis of correspondences—the multitude of correspondences possible in a poem, geological, cultural, historical, personal, in all directions but including the center. In another conversation, she told me, "the form crystallizes the sense." The exact word she used was "*sens*," which in French can mean most straightforwardly "sense," or less straightforwardly,

---

vii *"Notes on the Reversible Brocade," Wu Zetian,* Wild Geese Returning: Chinese Reversible Poems, *Michèle Métail, translated by Jody Gladding, NYRB, 2017, pg. 10.*

"meaning." And I have turned this phrase over often in my head since then to understand how poetic content (or sense, or meaning) is so complexly linked to its manifestation, shape, form. But I was to discover while translating *Les horizons du sol* that her choice of the word "crystallized" was also important—the concept of the crystal, as a structure that self-accumulates in form, is important to understanding Métail, who is also one of the very rare writers on either side of the Atlantic Ocean to write creatively of and into geology, landscape and location, and our situation within our place. In fact, many of her works, such as *Les horizons du sol*, are attached specifically to the site in which they were written or performed. (Other site-specific books of Métail's include *Toponyme : Berlin. Dédale-cadastre-jumelage-panorama*; *La route de cinq pieds*; *64 poèmes du ciel et de la terre (les métriques paysagères.)*; and facets of *Gigantextes*, a text variously performed/published outside the form of a book.) So, crystallize may also be interpreted geologically in that the poem takes on crystalline shape, fractally assembling around itself a form inseparable from its content. But also, word as crystal—as I found during translating certain words within *Les horizons du sol* that at first seemed resistant, untranslatable, but would, upon excavation, yield extraordinary resonances. I started to think of these terms somewhat like fossils as the way early naturalists might have seen them—as still moments within strata, placed to evoke reflection upon the creation occurring all about them. These were words like *terraqué*, which I discovered was the title of Breton poet Eugene Guillevec's first book, and which tormented me in its untranslatable sense of trembling between earth and water. Or words like *septentrional*, which my translation programs all stupidly translated as meaning only "north," until I finally discovered an exact equivalent in English, which opened to a vast history of meaning "of the north," or "boreal," and used on early maps, as well as to indicate the seven stars of Ursa Major. Then, strangely enough, I discovered Stephane Mallarmé also refers to the "Septentrion" in *Un coup de dés*, leading in turn to the concept of Mallarmé's CONSTELLATION, as discussed in Quentin Meillassoux's book *The Number and the Siren*, a discussion that seems particularly appropriate to *Les horizons du sol*, which tracks the close-to-incomprehensible span of the geological formation of Marseille through its human history to the "immemorial present," as well:

> "Now we know. . . that the author of the *Coup de dés* held the stars in their pure dissemination to be a celestial symbol of Chance. To cut out, with the gaze, a constellation from this senseless splendor, is to carry out an act wholly analogous to the poetic act according to Mallarmé."[viii]

In a sense, or *sens*, the complex constraint-content relationship that Métail has developed in her work, is cutting out that constellation from "senseless splendor"—giving sense/sens, or shape, or form, to an almost infinite spread of possibility.

Les horizons du sol was written during a three-month residency in Marseille at the centre international de poesie Marseille (CipM),

---

viii The Number and the Siren: A Decipherment of Mallarmé's Coup de dés, *Quentin Meillassoux, translated by Robin MacKay, Urbanomic Sequence, 2012, pg. 46.*

which then published *Les horizons du sol* through their *spectres familiers* series in 1999. *Les horizons du sol* is written in an immediately visible constraint of forty-eight characters per line, twenty-four lines per page, and comprises one long sentence of continuous enjambment. It also includes collages created by Métail from the Cassini maps of France, which were the first detailed maps of France, completed over four generations of Cassinis. The numerical connection of the constraint to the Provençal alphabet is slightly off—Provençal contains twenty-five letters, not twenty-four—but the shapeliness of the 24:48 ratio appealed to Métail (who was also forty-eight the year she wrote the piece). While the text may look "visual" (some early readers have compared its look to paintings, while others have compared it to boxes), and first read as obdurate and even abstract, it is upon closer engagement, rich and detailed, with an ongoing evolution that unfolds through deep geological time to botanical time into human-scale history, arriving at last to the "immemorial" present, the timeless point of now.

Métail asked me to retain her constraints in English, in order to convey the complete concept of *Les horizons du sol*, but also to convey her life's work of exploring that axis of correspondences between form and content. I understood that any translation that did not retain her original form would not be a translation at all, nor even a creative approximation. However, that didn't mean it was easy. English is a more concise language than French, which meant I was usually running at twenty-two lines per page compared to the twenty-four of the original. So, I followed the elaborate sentence structures of French perhaps a little more than in your usual

standard French-to-English translation, including more preposi-
tions and articles than I usually prefer to use. In other words, a
"toothbrush" would become "the brush of the teeth," but then I
don't mind the slightly awkward tone of some translations—I liked
having that sense of the original texture, rather than the sense of
forcing something into (questionable) American vernacular. With
that in mind, I also kept many site-specific references, particularly
geological ones, which didn't have an equivalent in an American
landscape. I did occasionally delight in English's more connotative
qualities—sometimes rendering an overly denotative term into
something more multitudinous. I also allowed myself to enter the
rare grammatical gray space—such as sneaking a "which" instead
of a "that" in order to reach the forty-eight characters each line de-
manded (I hope readers will forgive me). Overall, though, I limited
shortcuts as much as possible in my effort to understand the text,
which of course, I never fully will. Despite translating *Les horizons
du sol* across an ocean, and over way too much time, I still felt im-
mensely close to Métail and her work over the years it took me to
complete it. Her presence was always profoundly felt in the work
she had asked me to respect in form and content, and in the words
she used that opened onto worlds. While I will never fully finish
translating *Les horizons du sol*, its essential incompletion leaves it
open and evolving, I hope for all who read it too.

Many thanks to those who helped with the completion of this
translation, either through space, money, knowledge, or the ability
to speak and read French better than me: Michel Durand, Olivier
Brossard, PEN America, and the Lower Manhattan Cultural Council.

And to the editors of the following journals who published excerpts: the *Nation, Asymptote, Seedings,* and *River Rail,* and to Linda Russo and Marthe Reed for including my piece on the term *terraqué* in *Counter-Desecration: A Glossary for Writing Within the Anthropocene.* To John Yau for so generously publishing this translation—I couldn't hope for a better home for it. Thank you to Emmanuel Ponsart, Michaël Battalla and David Lespiau at cipM for their generosity and help with reprinting the original. And, thank you to Michèle Métail for her patience, generosity and her extraordinary constellation of creation.

—Marcella Durand

EARTH'S HORIZONS
PANORAMA

To that one nearby

AN OBSERVER LIMITS HER POINT OF VIEW TO THE LINE

OF A FOLD BORN FROM TORSIONS OF A GEOLOGICAL AGE TOO ANCIENT TO RESIST THE TRANSITIVE EARTHQUAKES CAUSING PLATES TO TREMBLE UNTIL INVASIVE UPLIFTS RESIST PRESSURES FROM A TERRAIN VERY TERRESTRIAL OF CRUST WHOSE SMOOTH BENDING STRETCH FORCES THE DOME OF THE BOW INTO AN INFLECTION AND GLACIALLY SUPERPOSES THE MOTIONS OF ARCHING AS THE REVERSE STRATIFICATION MOVEMENTS OF INTERLACING ELEMENTS BIND THE INCONSTANT AGGLUTINATES INTO DISCORDANT DEPOSITS UNDER LATERAL PRESSURE IN THE TORMENTED ZONE OF STRIATIONS IN WEIGHTY LAYERS OF REPLICAS AND FLOOD WAVE-CUT PLATFORMS THAT ACCENTUATE THE FLEXURE WITHOUT BREAKING ITS LAYERS CONSOLIDATED AT THE BASE BY A PROFUSION OF INVISIBLE ORGANICS THAT INSUBSTANTIAL AND TRANSITIVE PROJECTIONS OF TURBULENCES CONCENTRATE IN SOMBRE FRAGMENTS THAT DETACH UPON CONTACT WITH THE CRYSTALLIZATIONS OF THE DIVIDED GLOBE THAT THE SLOW START DISMANTLED CAUSING SUFFERING THROUGH FAST TRANSLATION AFTER TEMPORARY FLUCTUATIONS AFFECTED BY UNPREDICTABLE DEFORMATIONS WHOSE CRASHINGS CEASE JUST WHEN THE PEACEFUL SIMULACRUM OF A REMISSION COMMENCES NOT LIKE YESTERDAY WHEN EQUILIBRIUMS RUPTURED AT THE ABANDONED SPACE IN A DARK FRACTURE OF ITS PLINTH

AND THUS COMMENCES THE METAMORPHOSIS OF A RELIEF
MODELLING ITSELF AFTER THE VOLITION OF CONTRASTS
FOLLOWING THE MONOTONOUS CYCLE OF EROSION DEEPLY
UNDERLINING THE INTENSE ACTIONS OF A FRAGMENTING
PROCESS CONTINUOUSLY ALTERING BRITTLE FORMS THAT
ARE BLUNTED BY THE ASSAULTS OF TORRENTIALS WHOSE
EFFLUENT REDISTRIBUTES NAKED CRACKED SLOPES THAT
DISLOCATE UNTIL AN UNDERLYING GANGUE OF UNCOMMON
INTRUSIONS DETACHES ITSELF FROM A VEIN TO SMOOTH
OVER THE ROUGH SURFACES OF A WAVE OF SEDIMENTARY
STONES DEPOSITED UPON AND WHICH ACCUMULATED OVER
THE PROVISIONAL FOUNDATIONS OF A LAYER ON TOP OF
WHICH A NEW PILE IS HOLLOWED BY PLUMMETING ROCKS
THAT THE TUMBLE NO LONGER HOLDS SOLID AND SHIFTS
IN ENORMOUS OVERTHRUSTS ABANDONING THE RESIDUALS
AS LONG THREADS THAT DETACH AT THE SAME LEVEL AS
TRUNCATIONS OF WHICH AN IRREVERSIBLE DEGRADATION
EFFECTED BY TOPOGRAPHICAL CONFIGURATIONS ALREADY
EXCAVATING AN UNLEVELING THAT AN UNCEASING BASIN
WORKED OVER BY CORROSIVE ACID ERASES IN FAVOR OF
A PERISHABLE LAPSE WHICH GUARANTEES IN DISTENDED
INTERVALS A HYPOTHESIZED DURATION WHICH MOBILITY
REFLECTS IN AN UNCERTAIN TIME FRAME THAT RETURNS
AN ILLUSIONARY EVENTUALITY OF A DEFINITIVE STATE

ALTHOUGH THE MASSIF CONTINUALLY RECOILS FROM THE PRIMITIVE EXTENSIONS THAT CULMINATE ON IDENTICAL SIDES OF AMPLE SUMMIT RIDGES WITH ROUND OUTLINES INCLINED NORTH TOWARD DEPRESSED AREAS OF ERRATIC CONVERGENCES OF SCREE THAT MOUNTAINSIDES ABANDON TO THE PROFIT OF CRESTS MORE ACCIDENTAL IN THEIR CREATION AS THEY DIVIDE EXUBERANT WATERS FRAYING OVER TERRACED FOOTHILLS WHERE UNDULATING HEIGHTS CLUMSILY DRAW TRAILS THAT DISAPPEAR ON THE FLANK OF THE VALLEY'S OPAQUE AND MYSTERIOUS NORTH SIDE COVERED BY THE EYRIE OF FIERCE VEGETATION ROOTED IN THE STONY ARIDITY OF INCANDESCENT SCRUB WHICH SUDDENLY IGNITES THE FIREBREAK WHEN A DESSICATED FOOTPATH DEFEATED BY ITS OWN MEANDERING TURNS IN THE DIRECTION OF RAVINES CRISSCROSSED BY FURROWS THAT EXTEND PRECIPITOUS GRADIENTS DOWNWARD ALONG THE SURFACES OF OCHRE-COLORED WALLS WITHOUT SOIL TO COVER AND CONCEAL THE ROCKSTREWN DEBRIS WHICH DOMINATES THE RAWBONED PHYSIOGNOMIES REMINISCENT OF DESERTS OF WHICH EVERY EXTREMITY POSTULATES A HORIZON BECAUSE AT THAT DISTANCE A MIRAGE OF THE LANDSCAPE WILL NOT CONTINUE BEYOND THE GRADUALLY INCREASING FUZZINESS OF THE FROZEN ELEVATIONS AT THE FLOWER OF THE BORDER ON THE TRENCH'S EDGE OF

EPHEMERALS TORMENTED BY THE ABRUPT WHERE OBLIQUE STRIATIONS OF EXTRAORDINARILY FINE BEVELLING ARE TWISTED AFTER THEY PLUNGE INTO THE WHITE OF WORN LIMESTONE AND WHICH THEN DISINTEGRATE INTO LEVEL GROUND WHERE THE SCATHING SCAR INITIATES A NOTCH AT THE FOOT OF THE CONGLOMERATE WHICH APPEARS ON THE HORIZON OVERLOOKING THE RUPTURES OF VERTICAL AND OPEN LIPS WHERE ATMOSPHERES RUSH WITH SHOVES REPEATEDLY VIVACIOUSLY INTENSIFYING INDENTATIONS OF VALLEYS OFTEN INVADED EPISODICALLY DURING THE ASCENT BY INNER SEAS TO THE GAPING DOMAIN OF THE TEAR THAT WIDENED EXISTING CHANNELS THAT OXIDIZE CURIOUSLY REDDISH COULEES FOR MERGING WITHIN THE INTERSTICES OF THE PRECIOUS RUST ADDING COLOR TO THE WESTERN HORIZON THAT SUDDENLY INTENSIFIES IN EXTREMELY INTRICATE CONFINES OF SMALL AND STEEP-WALLED INLETS SO JAGGED THAT EACH OF THEIR ROCKY BRAIDS STICKS UP ABOVE THE TURBID WATER WHICH IN OVERFLOWING SUCCESSION SNEAKILY INFILTRATES TINY NETWORKS OF FISSURES AND AT THE SAME TIME DROWNS EACH TRACE OF FOUNDATIONAL ROCK WITH IMPRESSIONS OF FOSSILS STRANDED BY THE MAGMA INTRUSION WHILE NARROW CREEKS PERPETUATE A CONTEMPLATION OF ORES ALREADY MILLENNIAL EN FACE ARCHAIC TRANSGRESSION

OF THESE ENCLOSED TERRITORIES PETRIFIED BY DENSE
HAZARDS OF INDENTATIONS SWALLOWED BY WATER CLOSE
TO AN EMERGENT LAND MASS WHERE AN OBTRUSIVE CORD
TIES ITSELF INTO LESIONS WROUGHT BY OBSTACLES OF
BLEACHED DROSS ON THE BUTTE OF THE STARK COASTAL
DECOUPAGE CUT BY THE MATTER OF OTHER CONCRETIONS
OF MULTIPLE MINERALS SWEPT AWAY LITTLE BY LITTLE
BY VORTEXES ALONG AN ERODING SHORE WITH A POROUS
AND TROUBLED CRUST DISPERSED BY AIR WELL AND FAR
AWAY WITH ITS WEIGHT SUPPLEMENTED BY A LABORIOUS
GRAVITY OF RUSHING WAVES THAT FOLLOW A POTENTIAL
TRAJECTORY OF SUBSTANTIAL SHOALS ASCENDING ALONG
A PRECIPITOUS ESCARPMENT WHERE THE CONTINUITY OF
INDECOMPOSABLE MATERIALS IS THUS DISTINGUISHABLE
LIKE A SINGLE BODY THAT CAN NOT HINDER INCESSANT
LIQUID IN SPITE OF THE MECHANICAL AND REPETITIVE
UNDULATIONS WHOSE PROPAGATION IS REINFORCED BY A
METEORIC INFLUENCE THAT PRECIPITATES AGAINST THE
CLIFFS WITH THE SPEED OF FORTUITOUS CHRONOLOGIES
PASSING WITHIN EXPANDING REFERENCES WITHOUT EVER
MOLLIFYING EXCEPT WHEN THE EVAPORATION SATURATES
THE HYDRATION OF FROTHY AND UNVARYING NEBULOSITY
DURING ITS PROGRESSION OVER THE FORESHORE AT THE
JUNCTION OF TRIPLE SPHERES EXHAUSTING THE SPRING

UNDER THE TERRAIN OF WAVES OF WASHED-OUT ABYSSES
INSCRIBED BY SEAS SURROUNDING A FALLOW CONTINENT
WHOSE ENVELOPING SHORES DISINTEGRATE UNTIL SMALL
STATIONARY OBJECTS RELEASE UNEXPLORABLE CADENCED
AND CONCENTRIC VIBRATIONS THAT ARE NEITHER ALIVE
NOR PLACATED AND THAT RETURN A UNIQUE SONAR ECHO
OF HYPOTHETICAL DENSITIES SOLELY VERIFIABLE THRU
EXPERIMENTAL CONJECTURES AS EVIDENCED BY EXPANSE
OF LAND WHICH MANIFESTED EARLY OVER AN ENGULFING
MANTLE AT THE TURNING POINT OF COAGULATING TO AN
EQUILIBRIUM OF REACTIVATED ALTERNATIVES REJECTED
AT PROFOUND DEPTHS AND REMODELED WITH THE PROPER
INVERSION OF MECHANISMS FROM AN ANTERIOR TIME OF
A GASH WHICH EXUDING AND ENDURES VOLCANIC MAGMAS
WHEN THE DORSAL IMMERSION ATTACK ON THE SECTIONS
THAT ARE ACTIVE TEARS AT THE BORDERS OF WIDENING
GRAVES THAT REFORM THEMSELVES AS ABYSSES PUSHING
UP TO THE SUBSOIL VIA THE NODAL PROPAGATED UNDER
AN IMPETUS OF ACOUSTICS AND COMPLICATED REMANENT
MAGNETIZATION THAT PERMITS DISCOVERING AN ISLAND
HOVERING LIKE A SHIPWRECK PRIED OUT OF THE EARTH
SO THAT PROXIMITY'S BEACON IS TOUGH TO DETECT ON
SUBMERGED SHOALS WHICH DURING THE NIGHT MASK THE
ANXIETY OF A WORLD HELD BETWEEN GROUND AND WATER

IN A CIRCUMFERENCE'S TURN MARKED BY THE CARDINAL
DIRECTIONS SPONTANEOUSLY ANIMATED BY THE EXTREME
DIVERSITY OF ORIENTATIONS SITUATED DIAMETRICALLY
THAT DISAPPEAR DUE TO THE INACCESSIBLE DISTANCES
OF ANTIPODES IMPLANTED LIKE SO MANY ARCHIPELAGOS
WITHOUT DESTINATION ALTHOUGH THE ROTUNDITY OF AN
ODYSSEY CIRCUMSCRIBED WITHIN CIRCULARITY MANAGES
TO BREAK THROUGH A CROSSING GUIDED BY THE ARC OF
MERIDIAN SHADOWS WHOSE ORIENTATION DECIDES WHICH
ABERRATIONS WILL DIVIDE THE SUNDIAL'S MEASURE OF
DIFFRACTED MAGNETIZATION WHEN SURRENDER TO EVERY
NAVIGATION THROUGH THE STRAIT OF HOLES CHARTERED
BY THE ORBITING AND ECLIPSED COSMOGRAPHICS WHICH
REGULATE THE UNDERTOW'S ITINERARY OF DISTORTIONS
OF THE MAGNETIC POLES WHERE LOW PRESSURE SYSTEMS
FLOUT THE FOCAL DISTANCES OF WEATHER IN CYCLONIC
LATITUDES WHERE PERTURBATIONS SWEEPING IN BURSTS
EXCEED THE VORTEX AND RICOCHET UPON THE LANCE OF
MANEUVERS WHERE THE RETURN TO THE COAST BLAZES A
SHARPENED OSCILLATION THAT DISTORTS ITS REVERSED
APPROACH WHOSE SPEED IS SUSTAINED BY THE CERTAIN
DECLINATION OF THE PROMONTORY AHEAD OF ANCHORING
UPON THE CONTINENTAL FREEBOARD AS THE LIGHTHOUSE
BURSTS SEAMARKS IN MAGNITUDES CLOSE TO ITS LIMIT

VIA DAY OF VIOLENT WIND THREATENING INTERMITTENT TEMPESTS WHILE BAROMETERS ABRUPTLY TUMBLE THUSLY THWARTING ANY POSSIBLE FORECAST OF THE MOMENTARY FRONT OF A QUASI-ARCTIC THERMAL DETERIORATION OF WHICH CONDENSES VAPORS EXHALED BY SEPTENTRIONALS ALONG THE GRADIENT OF THE CREVASSE THAT ENGENDER A MAGISTERIAL TRANSFORMATION OF GNARLS TO SPACES OF CALM PASSAGE THAT DIMINISH THROUGH THE LOCH'S DIVISION OF ONE MILLION NAUTICAL FLAGS UNFOLDING DESPITE BALLAST CRASHING DOWN AMID STRENGTHENING SQUALLS SWERVING IMPETUOUSLY AND RELEASING SPRAY IN AN AGGRESSIVE BREEZE WHICH FORECASTS IMMINENT CHANGE WHILE INCREASING IN A REVOLUTION PARALLEL TO THE PLANETARY CAMBER DECELERATING DUE TO THAT ROTATING INFLUENCE OF FRICTION AGAINST WHICH ITS PARAMETERS RESIST AND WITH WHICH AN EXCRUCIATING SLIPPAGE COLLIDES AS SOON AS THE WRINKLES IN THE DIMENSIONS OF ISOBARS ARE ASSESSED OUTSIDE OF AN ORDINARY LULL AND THE ATTEMPT IS MADE TO SUCCEED AT SUCH A CROSSING AFTER A SHIP LAUNCHES WITHOUT ANY DREAD OF PROVOKING THE SHIPWRECKED PERILS OF AVARICE AWAKENED AT ANCHORAGE BY WAVES REVERSING CONTRARY TO THE BREAKS IN THE SHORE OF FRACTURED ANFRACTUOSITIES STRUCK UNDER BY THE SURF'S SHOCK

TRACES AN IMAGINARY LINE BETWEEN FLUX AND REFLUX
THAT THE STANDARD CURVE IN LEGITIMATE PROTRUSION
OPENS TO A STORMY SEA OF SWELLING TURBULENCES IN
SAME MEASURE OF CONJUNCTIONS THAT RHYME IN EXACT
AMPLITUDE OF LAYER AS AN INSTANTANEOUS INTENTION
NECESSITATES AN ADJUSTMENT TO SCALE REDUCED BY A
DEVIATION THAT A FIXED SIGNAL AFTER AN ELEVATION
APPROXIMATE TO NUMEROUS POINTS ON THE HORIZONTAL
SURFACE OF AN ARBITRARY MEAN COMPENSATES FOR THE
EDGE VISIBLE THANKS TO A SHEER GRADATION DURABLY
REGULATED BY A MAREOGRAPH WHICH CONTROLS FOR THE
INCOMMENSURABLE WHILE UNEASILY RECORDING ITS OWN
MATERIAL VARIATIONS WITHOUT POWER TO INFLUENCE A
LOGIC THAT ATTRACTS BEFORE ALL AN IMAGE CODIFIED
BY A REPRESENTATION IGNORANT OF THE VERY FRAGILE
SENSATION OF EQUILIBRIUM BETWEEN ABOVE AND BELOW
OF WHOSE DIFFERENCE MAKES PERCEIVABLE AGAIN THAT
UNITY OF AN ABSENCE REVEALED AS SNEAKILY FANNING
FEAR OF THE VOID IN INFINITE GRANDEUR GENERATING
TRUE TENSION WHEN COHERENCE OF A RIGID STABILITY
RUPTURES FROM THE EFFECT OF OSCILLATORY DYNAMICS
OF WHICH THE COEFFICIENT IS IN PROPORTION TO THE
REAL ATTRACTION WHICH THAT FRUITLESS AXIS EXERTS
UPON THE SOMEWHAT CONSIDERABLE DIMENSION OF ZERO

IN THE SERVICE OF THE FIGURE WHICH SCRAMBLES THE BRIGHT SIGN OF FREQUENCIES STILL ASSOCIATED WITH OVERLY BUCCAL VOWELS BUT THROUGH TRANSPOSING THE INTELLIGIBLES WHICH FOR THEIR PART FORM VARIANTS OF A NUMERIC TEXT IN WHICH SERIES OF COLUMNS ARE ALIGNED AND WHERE LIGATURES ADOPT THE APPEARANCE OF LACUNAE VIA THE ARTIFICES OF THE CONVENTIONAL WHILE THE MESSAGE TRANSFORMS IN THE MARGINS OF A CODE THAT REDUCES THE DISPROPORTION OF ANNOUNCED PLAUSIBLES IN ALPHABETICAL COMBINATION WHAT MUST BE SUBSTITUTED ONE FOR THE OTHER BEFORE REVISION INTO POSITIONS MARKED BY CERTAIN CLASSIFIED KEYS ABBREVIATED TO INITIALS OF THE NAME THAT CAREFUL VERIFICATION BETRAYS TO THE RISK OF THE POSSIBLE CONFUSION WITH INCOHERENCIES ASSEMBLED UNDER THE RUSE OF INACCURATE SEQUENCES WHOSE HESITANT DEBT JUSTIFIES THE VERY EXACT TERMS OF DELICATE WORDS TO BE AUTHENTICATED IN ORDER NOT TO DISCLOSE THE CRYPTOGRAM AS A PARODY OF CALCULATION PERILOUSLY DRAFTED IN THE EVENT OF RUSHING WITHOUT A LETTER TRANSMITTED BY THE DECIPHERER COMPLETELY MASKING THE PERMUTATED AND SECRET CORRESPONDENCES OF THE WRITING WHICH STRATEGICALLY CONCEALED WITHIN THE COMPOSITION IS ISOLATED BY LAW FROM THE INTERIOR

THIS DEAD ANGLE BASTION IN WHICH A PAGE PERSISTS BENEATH SEALS CAUGHT WITHIN THEIR IMPRESSIONS OF MISTAKES ALONG WITH AN OMISSION ANTICIPATED SANS THE SIGNAL OF THE LIGHTHOUSE AT THE FIRST FUTILE ALERT OF AN ARSENAL OF THE SPIRIT IN POSITION AS SOON AS NIGHT LOCKS ITS RAMPART LINED BY CRENELS ALONG A SURROUNDING WALL BOUNDARIED BY OBSERVANT PATROLS OF AN INVESTIGATION THAT HOLLOWS OUT THE LINE OF REINFORCING STRUCTURES SHOOTING DIRECTLY TO A RECTILINEAR RADIUS IN WHICH AN ARROW POINTS IN A GRAPHIC DIRECTION TO LINEAMENTS OF SYLLABIC CONTOURS PIERCED BY LOOPHOLES NO SOONER CUT INTO THE THICKNESS OF A VIGIL DEFENDING ACCESS TO ITS ESSENTIAL FLANKS THAN A RUDE PROTOCOL FOLLOWS OF WHICH THE REPETITION ENGAGING TOWARD THE CENTRAL POSITION OF ORAL FORMULAE SEQUESTERED WITHIN THE FORTIFICATIONS OF LYRICS WHICH DETAIN INEFFABLES OFTEN REBELLIOUS TO INSURGENT SUBJECT AND TRYING TO PROTECT ITSELF FULLY AGAINST LISTENING AT THE THRESHOLD OF DETECTING DANGERS RECOGNIZABLE UPON ONE'S GUARD WITH ALL THE MOVEMENT OF A FALSIFIED INTERROGATION CONTAINED WITHIN THE COLLECTION OF EVIDENCE WRITTEN ONLY ON THE FINAL PAGE OF FACTS OBSERVED BY THE LOOKOUT WHO WATCHES ON THE MOUNT

TAKEN BY PLUNGING PERSPECTIVES WHERE IMAGINABLES
ABSCOND LOSING ACUITY NO SOONER THAN THE EYE AND
ITS ANNEXES WANDERING THE QUADRILLAGE TESTIFY TO
A CHAIN OF COINCIDENCE TO WHICH A SURVEY IMPARTS
A LEGEND SO THAT LOCAL EQUIDISTANCES BENEATH THE
CROSSHATCHING OF DIMINUTIONS AT THE INTERSECTION
OF BITUMINOUS SEGMENTS CONNECTED ACROSS BEAMS IN
SHRINKING SOLIDARITY WITH STEPS SHAPED BY DOUBLY
STAGED STAIRWAYS WHOSE RAMPS RUN STRAIGHT TO THE
HEART OF ROTARIES UNDERSCORING A DIVISION IN THE
MEASUREMENTS OF DEGREES TOWARD THE ALLEY LEADING
TO AN AREA EVEN MORE BURDENED BY ROADS SATURATED
WITH A SQUEEZING URBANIZATION WHERE WANDERING IN
PURSUIT OF ITS MOST INTIMATE IMPASSES KEEPS RAGE
ON WALLS LARGELY CONFINED ONTO CRACKING EXPANSES
TO THE PINION WHEN THE FRAMING OF RIGHTS IMPOSES
CAVALIER VISUALS THAT READ SYMMETRICAL AS OPTICS
OF A RETICULAR ILLUSION PROJECTED ON A LABYRINTH
DEVISED TO PLANT MILESTONES IN THE AGGLOMERATION
OF THE EXPIRING TEXTURE OF A CADASTRAL MAP WHICH
REVEALS NEVERTHELESS SOLIDLY AGRARIAN LAND WHOSE
CADASTRAL PARCELS MUST BE EXACTLY LOCATED BEFORE
SKETCHING OUT THE PLAN FOR APPROACHING EVEN MORE
SCRUPULOUSLY THE PURITY OF A CITY WITHOUT A NAME

ALWAYS LATENT IN ITS INDEPENDENCE ENCROACHING ON IMPERIALIST EXCESS FROM WHERE THE TYRANNIES LASH OUT AGAINST OUTRIDERS WHO ENSEMBLE ARE ONLY JUST SUBMISSIVE WHEN CHASTISING ABUSERS ARE COMPELLED TO REPENT FOR A WICKED LIFE IN WHICH FANATICISTS SUBJECT EVERY LIAISON TO THE CAUSE AND EFFECT OF CRYING OUTSIDE MEA CULPA LIKE A BITTER ATONEMENT BY CAPTIVES WHOSE YOKES JAR THE INTOLERABLES WHO FORCE THE DISHONOR OF MORALITY AS CRUELLY AS THE EXPULSION OF INDIGENTS FROM REFUGE RELEASED FROM LANGUAGE OF FLESHY VERNACULARS SLAMMING DOWN THE PASSAGE OF INVECTIVES AND BRAVING REPRESSIONS SO VIOLENTLY AFTER ESCAPING SUFFOCATION OF PAPILLAE BENEATH A GAG OF EXPRESSION WITH AN OVERWHELMING SENSE OF FAILURE WHEN FOLLY OF THE NARROW-MINDED OVERWORKS THOSE WHO ARE HYPERTROPHIED IMPRISONED WITHIN THE TWISTED PARTITIONING BETWEEN MODES OF SPEAKING THAT EXCLUDE CRAMPED PHRASES PRESSURING THE PRONOUNCEMENTS FROM THE OTHER PART HAMPERING AN EFFUSION OF SAYINGS OF WHICH THE SAID IMPEDES ANY HESITATION IN LOOSENING FRANK TONGUES EXCEPT WHEN THE UNSPOKEN OF ENFRANCHISED SYNTAX REVOLTS AT STRIVING FOR EVERYTHING ONLY TO DISCOVER WITH THE OBVERSE OF ERASURE THE MOST FINAL OF PHRASES

TO THE GLORIOUS MEMORY OF COMMEMORATIVES THAT IN GRAVE TOPNOTES SING OF THE VANISHING REMEMBRANCE OF THE VERY FINAL DATE WITHIN A CHRONOLOGY WHOSE SANCTIFIED INDETERMINATION OF BYGONES LESS EXACT IN THEIR CHANGES BUT MORE PROPITIOUS IN REVIVING THE EPHEMERIDES ABANDONED TO THE POWER OF RECALL THAT WHICH FORGOTTEN IN A RECOLLECTION INSCRIBED ON THE FRONTON OF CORBELLED CORNICE WITH CONCISE EX-VOTO ON REVERSE AGAIN CAUGHT BY PHENOMENAE OF TENACIOUS YET DISTANT MEMORIES AND UNDULY FILLED WITH UNCERTAINTY AS TO THE AUTHENTICITY OF THOSE FABULOUS VESTIGES OF THE AFTERIMAGES ASSIMILATED IN AN ANALOGY OF REMINISCING ABOUT A NOW EXTINCT PAST THAT DOES NOT PERSIST IN THE MINDS OF THOSE WHO AID THE ARCHIVING OF APPRECIATIONS ACCORDING TO THE BARELY OBJECTIVE CONCORDANCES ON ANTERIOR MONUMENTS ALIGNED WITH ANNALS SOMETIMES AMNESIAC ON HARDLY OBSOLETE TWISTS OF HISTORY OMITTED BIT BY BIT FROM ANTIQUE EXCAVATIONS IN THE DEBRIS OF DIGS TO RETRIEVE OBSOLETE LIVES DIGNIFIED BY THE RELENTLESS RECOLLECTIONS HAUNTING THE OPPRESSIVE MNEMONICS THUS AN INTRUSIVE NARRATOR EXACERBATES THE PERCEPTIVES OCCUPIED WITH SCRUTINIZING A SKY OPENING TO THE PERPETUITY OF AN IMMEMORIAL SOUTH

LEGEND

Earth's horizon: Accumulation of elements within a geological layer. So this collection, invented by successive contributions, mixes very diverse elements.

Caliber of texts: It follows the number of letters in the Provençal alphabet.

The material of collages: The collages come from Cassini's map (18th century), which is so close to writing in its use of the line. The image is a poem.

The littoral city: It is situated at the point of contact between the lithosphere, the atmosphere and the hydrosphere.

Panorama: Visual field / semantic field.

The transgression: The sea reclaims the "lost continent," the south-Provençal continent about which the geologists hypothesize.

The mareograph: Located along the Corniche, the mareograph, or tide gauge determines the national height or "levelling" of France. [The mareograph of Marseille measures changes in sea levels, which is used to determine the "zero level" for France; the Corniche is a road that winds along the Mediterranean]

The cipher's service: Charged with transmitting secret messages from Fort Saint-Nicolas. [Louis the XIV had the Fort Saint-Nicolas built to protect the harbor of Marseille.]

The hill of the guard: Ancient location of a lookout.

The magistral: Master wind, "mistral" in Provençal.

The names of places: The barrier of the firewall, the island plane, the impasse of intimates, the street of honors (anc. dishonor), the refuge.

Inscriptions: Raised upon monuments, plaques. One day in a violent wind. . . (escalator of the stock exchange); the monument to the Great Confinement (Vieille Charité [a former almshouse]); to the glorious memory. . . (Pierre Dessemond Street).

Historic allusions: "the city without a name"; "the always latent independence of the city."

LES HORIZONS DU SOL
PANORAMA

à celui de l'auprès

Michèle Métail

LES HORIZONS DU SOL
PANORAMA

'''Le Refuge'''

cip*M* / Spectres Familiers

L'OBSERVATEUR LIMITE SON POINT DE VUE À LA LIGNE

L'OBSERVATEUR LIMITE SON POINT DE VUE À LA LIGNE

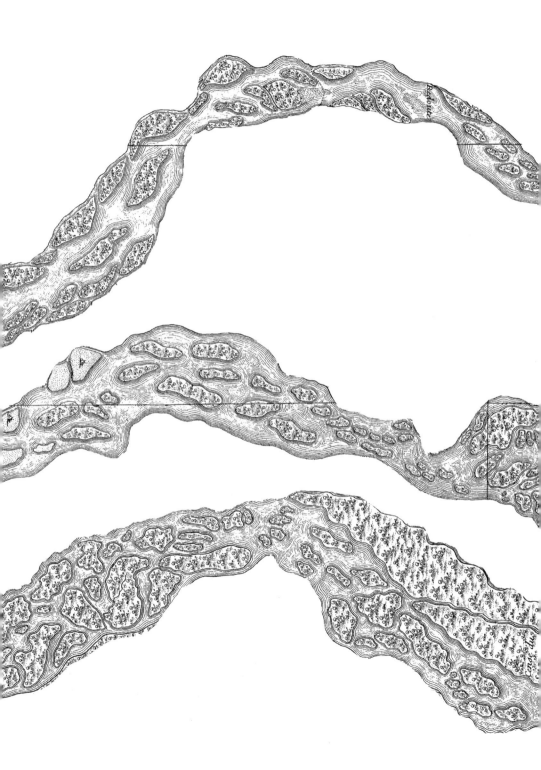

DU PLI NAISSANT DES TORSIONS D'UN ÂGE GÉOLOGIQUE
TROP ANCIEN POUR RÉSISTER AUX SISMIQUES DÉCALÉES
QUI ÉBRANLENT LES PLAQUES JUSQU'À L'ENVAHISSANTE
SURRECTION REPOUSSANT LES TERRAINS SI TERRESTRES
DE LA CROÛTE DONT L'ÉTIREMENT LISSE INFLÉCHIT LA
COURBURE EN DÔME ET QUE SE SUPERPOSENT LENTEMENT
LES MOUVANTES ARQUÉES TANDIS QUE S'INVERSENT LES
STRATIFICATIONS AUX ÉLÉMENTS ENTRECROISÉS QUE LE
BASCULEMENT AGGLUTINE EN DÉPÔTS DISCORDANTS SOUS
LA PRESSION DE LATÉRALES DANS LA ZONE TOURMENTÉE
DES STRIURES QUI S'ÉTAGENT EN RÉPLIQUES PESANTES
ET DÉBORDENT SUR LES PLATES-FORMES ACCENTUANT LA
FLEXURE SANS BRISER SES COUCHES CONSOLIDÉES À LA
BASE PAR UN FOISONNEMENT D'ORGANIQUES INVISIBLES
QUE LES PROJECTIONS FLASQUES ET TRANSITOIRES DES
TURBULENCES CONCENTRENT EN LAMBEAUX SOMBRES D'OÙ
SE DÉTACHENT PAR CONTACT LES CRISTALLISATIONS DU
GLOBE MORCELÉ QUE LE SURSAUT TARDIF DÉMANTÈLE EN
LUI FAISANT SUBIR UNE FURIEUSE TRANSLATION SELON
DES PHASES TEMPORAIRES AFFECTÉES D'IMPRÉVISIBLES
DÉFORMATIONS DONT LES COLLISIONS CESSENT DÈS QUE
S'AMORCE LE TRANQUILLE SIMULACRE D'UNE RÉMISSION
NE LAISSANT HIER APRÈS RUPTURE D'ÉQUILIBRE QU'UN
ESPACE ABANDONNÉ À LA CASSURE NOIRE DE SON SOCLE

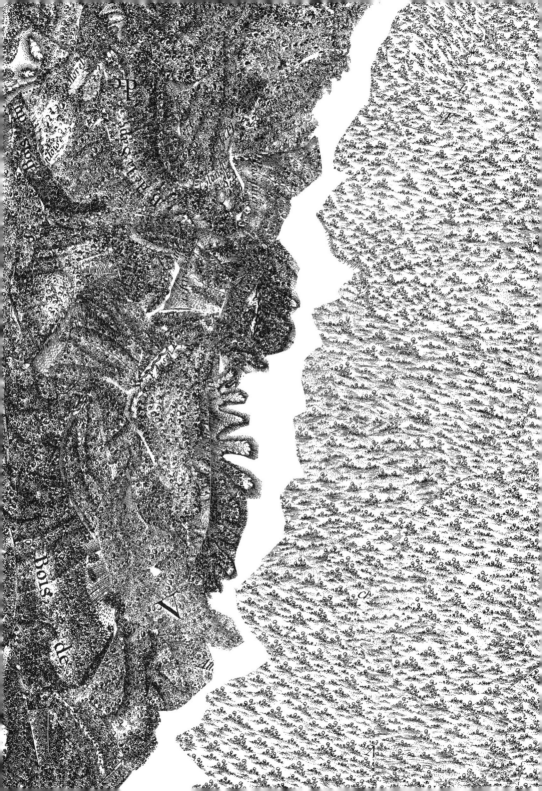

ALORS QUE COMMENCE LA MÉTAMORPHOSE DU RELIEF QUI
SE MODÈLE AU GRÉ DES CONTRASTES SUIVANT LE CYCLE
MONOTONE DE L'USURE PROFONDE SOUS L'ACTION DENSE
DES PROCESSUS DE FRAGMENTATION QUI ALTÈRENT SANS
DISCONTINUER LES FORMES MOLLES ÉMOUSSÉES PAR LES
ATTAQUES DES TORRENTIELLES DONT L'ÉCOULEMENT MET
À NU LES PROFILS FRACTURÉS EN DISLOQUANT JUSQU'À
LA GANGUE LES RARES INTERCALATIONS SOUS-JACENTES
DÉGAGÉES DE LEURS GISEMENTS ET QUI S'APLANISSENT
ENTRAÎNANT TOUTES LES ASPÉRITÉS DANS LE FLOT DES
SÉDIMENTS QUI SE DÉPOSENT ET S'ACCUMULENT SUR LE
FOND PROVISOIRE D'UNE NAPPE OÙ DE NOUVEAU L'AMAS
S'ARASE EN SE CREUSANT D'ÉBOULIS QUE LA CHUTE NE
PARVIENT PLUS À STABILISER ET QUI SE DÉPLACE PAR
GRANDS CHARRIAGES ABANDONNANT DES RÉSIDUELS TOUT
AU LONG DE SES TARAUDAGES QUI DÉCHAUSSENT AU RAS
LES TRONCATURES DONT LA DÉGRADATION IRRÉVERSIBLE
CAUSE À LA CONFIGURATION DES TOPOGRAPHIQUES DÉJÀ
EXCAVÉES UNE DÉNIVELLATION BRUTALE QUE LE BASSIN
SANS CESSE RETRAVAILLÉ PAR DES CORROSIVES ACIDES
EFFACE À LA FAVEUR D'UN LAPS PÉRISSABLE ASSURANT
AUX INTERVALLES DISTENDUS UNE DURÉE SUPPOSÉE QUE
LA MOBILITÉ RÉPERCUTE À MARGE INCERTAINE RENDANT
BIEN ILLUSOIRE L'ÉVENTUALITÉ D'UN ÉTAT DÉFINITIF

MÊME SI LE MASSIF PERSISTE EN RECUL DES ÉTENDUES
PRIMITIVES QUI CULMINENT À LA COTE DES RELATIVES
D'OÙ S'ÉBAUCHENT LES CROUPES AUX SOMMETS EMPÂTÉS
DANS LEURS ARRONDIS QUI S'ABAISSENT VERS LE NORD
EN DÉPRESSION LIEU DE CONVERGENCE DES ERRATIQUES
ÉBOULÉS PAR BLOCS QUE LES VERSANTS DÉLAISSENT AU
PROFIT DES CRÊTES PLUS ACCIDENTÉES EN LEUR FAÎTE
LORSQU'ELLES PARTAGENT LES EAUX EXUBÉRANTES PUIS
S'EFFRANGENT SUR LES CONTREFORTS EN GRADINS D'OÙ
LES HAUTEURS VALLONNÉES DESSINENT MALADROITEMENT
LEURS RAIDILLONS DISPARAISSANT À FLANC DE L'UBAC
CONFUS ET IMPÉNÉTRABLE SOUS SON COUVERT À L'AIRE
FORT VÉGÉTALE ENRACINÉE DANS L'ARIDITÉ PIERREUSE
DE CES BROUSSAILLES INCANDESCENTES QUI EMBRASENT
VITE LA BARRIÈRE DU COUPE-FEU LORSQUE LE SENTIER
ASSÉCHÉ VAINCU PAR SES MÉANDRES SE DÉTOURNE VERS
LES RAVINES SILLONNÉES DE RIGOLES QUE PROLONGENT
LES DÉCLIVITÉS ENCAISSÉES ENTRE LES PAROIS OCRES
DE LA MURAILLE SANS HUMUS QUI SE REFERME SUR SES
RUINES ROCHEUSES OÙ PRÉDOMINENT LES PHYSIONOMIES
ANGULAIRES SEMBLABLES AUX DÉSERTIQUES DONT TOUTE
EXTRÊMITÉ SUPPOSE L'HORIZON CAR À CETTE DISTANCE
LE MIRAGE DE LA VUE NE PORTE PAS AU-DELÀ DU FLOU
GRADUEL DE LA DÉNIVELÉE FIGÉE À FLEUR DE LISIÈRE

SUR L'ARÊTE TRANCHÉE D'ÉPHÉMÈRES TOURMENTÉES PAR L'ABRUPT OÙ S'ENCHEVÊTRENT LES STRIES OBLIQUES À BISEAU TRÈS AMINCI LORSQU'ELLES PLONGENT DANS LE BLANC DES CALCAIRES RONGÉS QUI SE DÉLITENT PLATS SITÔT QUE L'ÉCORCHURE CINGLANTE ENTAME L'ENCOCHE AU PIED DU CONGLOMÉRAT QUI SE PROFILE EN AVANCÉE SURPLOMBLANT LES FAILLES AUX LÈVRES VERTICALES ET OUVERTES OÙ S'ENGOUFFRENT LES ATMOSPHÉRIQUES PAR POUSSÉES RÉPÉTÉES INTENSIFIANT AVEC VIVACITÉ LES ÉCHANCRURES DANS LES VALLÉES ENVAHIES LORS DE LA REMONTÉE SOUVENT ÉPISODIQUE DES MERS INTÉRIEURES AU DOMAINE BÉANT DE LA DÉCHIRURE SURCREUSANT LES CANNELURES QUI S'OXYDENT EN COULÉES CURIEUSEMENT ROUGEÂTRES POUR SE COMBINER DANS LES INTERSTICES AUX ROUILLURES PRÉCIEUSES COLORANT LES COUCHANTS DÈS QUE S'ENFLAMMENT SUBITEMENT LES CONFINS TRÈS INTRIQUÉS DES CALANQUES SI DÉCHIQUETÉES QUE TOUS LEURS FAISCEAUX S'ÉRIGENT HORS DES TURBIDITÉS EN SUCCESSIONS DÉBORDANTES QUI INFILTRENT DOUCEMENT LES MOINDRES RÉSEAUX DE FISSURES NOYANT MÊME LES TRACES DES SOUBASSEMENTS AUX EMPREINTES FOSSILES ÉCHOUÉES LÀ PAR INTRUSION TANDIS QUE DES CRIQUES ÉTROITES SE PERPÉTUE UNE CONTEMPLATION D'ORES ET DÉJÀ MILLÉNAIRE FACE À LA TRANSGRESSION SURANNÉE

Etang des Landes

Etang du Galejon

DE CES TERRITORIALES CLOSES PÉTRIFIÉES D'ÉCUEILS
COMPACTES AUX INDENTATIONS GORGÉES D'EAU PROCHES
DE L'ÉMERGENCE OÙ SE NOUE LE CORDON APPARENT DES
LÉSIONS TRAVAILLÉES PAR L'ACHOPPEMENT DES ÉCUMES
BLANCHÂTRES EN BUTTE AU MORNE DÉCOUPAGE LITTORAL
ÉRODANT LES AUTRES CONCRÉTIONS DE LEURS MATIÈRES
LES PLUS MINÉRALES ENTRAÎNÉES PEU À PEU DANS LES
TOURBILLONS DE CET AFFOUILLEMENT DÉCONCERTANT DE
L'ÉCORCE POREUSE QUE L'AIR EMPORTE LOIN BIEN QUE
SA PESANTEUR AJOUTE À LA GRAVITÉ DOULOUREUSE PAR
ACCÉLÉRATION DES DÉFERLANTES SUIVANT LA POSSIBLE
TRAJECTOIRE DE BRISANTS FOUDROYANTS QUI DÉRIVENT
LE LONG DU FRONT ESCARPÉ OÙ SE DÉMARQUE POURTANT
LA CONTINUITÉ DES INDÉCOMPOSABLES COMME UN CORPS
SIMPLE QUE NE PEUT ENTAILLER LE FLUIDE INCESSANT
MALGRÉ LA REDITE MÉCANIQUE DES ONDULATOIRES DONT
LA PROPAGATION ENCORE RENFORCÉE PAR UNE MOUVANCE
MÉTÉORIQUE SE PRÉCIPITE CONTRE LES FALAISES À LA
VITESSE DES CHRONOLOGIQUES FORTUITES QUI PASSENT
DANS DES REPÈRES EN EXPANSION SANS JAMAIS MOLLIR
SAUF QUAND L'ÉVAPORATION SATURE D'HYDRATATION LA
SUSPENSION DE NÉBULOSITÉS MOUTONNÉES INVARIABLES
DANS LEUR PROGRESSION SUR L'ESTRAN À LA JONCTION
DES SPHÈRES TRIPLES OÙ S'ÉPUISE LE RUISSELLEMENT

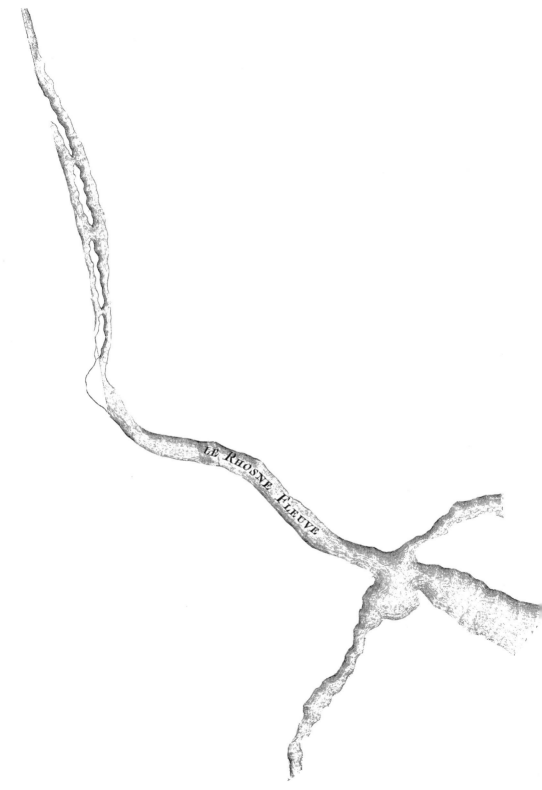

LE RHOSNE FLEUVE

SOUS LE TERRAIN DE VAGUES DES ABYSSALES DÉLAVÉES
INSCRITES AUX MARITIMES D'UN CONTINENT EN FRICHE
DONT LES RIVAGES RECOUVERTS S'AFFAISSENT JUSQU'À
L'INEXPLORABLE RELÂCHEMENT DES STATIONNAIRES PEU
CONCENTRIQUES DANS LEURS VIBRATIONS CADENCÉES NI
VIVES NI AMOLLIES ET QUI RENVOIENT L'ÉCHO UNIQUE
DU SONDAGE DE DENSITÉS HYPOTHÉTIQUES VÉRIFIABLES
PAR LES EXPÉRIMENTALES AUX CONJECTURES ÉVIDENTES
DE LA PRÉSENCE D'UN TERRITOIRE MANIFESTÉ TÔT SUR
LE MANTEAU DES ENGLOUTIS À LA CHARNIÈRE ÉPAISSIE
D'UN BALANCEMENT QUE LES ALTERNATIVES RÉACTIVÉES
REJETTENT PAR LES PROFONDEURS ET REMODÈLENT AVEC
L'INVERSION PROPRE AUX DISPOSITIFS D'UNE PÉRIODE
BIEN ANTÉRIEURE À L'ENTAILLE QUI SUINTE ET SUBIT
SES VOLCANIQUES QUAND L'ÉMERSION DORSALE ATTAQUE
DE SES ACTIVES LES PORTIONS DÉCHIQUETÉES AU BORD
DES FOSSES ÉVASÉES QUI SE RECONSTITUENT DANS LES
ABÎMES REPOUSSÉS JUSQU'AU TRÉFONDS PAR LA NODALE
PROPAGÉE SOUS L'IMPULSION DES ACOUSTIQUES ET QUE
COMPLEXE SA RÉMANENCE PERMET LA DÉCOUVERTE D'UNE
ÎLE PLANE COMME UNE ÉPAVE PRISE À LA TERRE ALORS
BALISE D'UNE PROXIMITÉ À PEINE DÉCELABLE SUR LES
HAUTS-FONDS SI SUBMERSIBLES QUE MASQUE DEPUIS LE
SOIR L'AGITATION ENCLAVÉE DANS UN MONDE TERRAQUÉ

SUD

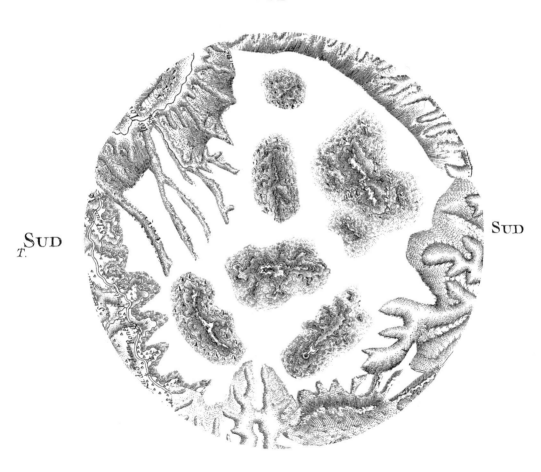

SUD

T. SUD

SUD

SUD

AU TOUR D'UNE CIRCONFÉRENCE DÉLIMITÉE AUX QUATRE
CARDINAUX PAR L'IMPROVISTE ANIMÉ DE LA PLURALITÉ
EXTRÊME DES ORIENTS SITUÉS EN DIAMÉTRALES QUE LA
RAISON ESTOMPE VERS LES LOINTAINES INACCESSIBLES
DES ANTIPODES IMPLANTÉS COMME AUTANT D'ARCHIPELS
SANS DESTINATION QUOIQUE LA ROTONDITÉ DU PÉRIPLE
CIRCONSCRIT AUX CIRCULAIRES MÉNAGE SES PERCÉES À
GUÉ GUIDÉE PAR L'ARC DES OMBRES MÉRIDIENNES DONT
L'ORIENTATION DÉTERMINE LES ABERRATIONS DIVISANT
LE CADRAN COMPASSÉ DE L'AIMANTÉE DÉVIÉE QUAND SE
LIVRE À L'ESTIME TOUTE NAVIGATION PAR LE DÉTROIT
DES TROUÉES AFFRÉTÉES AUX COSMOGRAPHIQUES TANTÔT
ORBITES TANTÔT ÉCLIPSES QUI RÈGLENT L'ITINÉRAIRE
À CONTRE-COURANT DES DISTORSIONS DES PÔLES OÙ SE
JOUENT LES DÉPRESSIONNAIRES FOCALES DE DISTANCES
MÉTÉO À LATITUDES CYCLONALES BALAYANT EN RAFALES
LES PERTURBATIONS AFIN DE DÉPASSER LES REMOUS ET
RICOCHER SUR LA LANCÉE DES MANŒUVRES AUXQUELLES
LE RETOUR DES CÔTIÈRES FRAYE UN ROULIS D'AFFILÉE
QUI FAUSSE CETTE APPROCHE À REBOURS QUE L'ALLURE
SOUTIENT NÉCESSAIREMENT PAR LA DÉCLINAISON DE LA
CERTITUDE DU CAP AVANT D'ATTEINDRE LE FRANC-BORD
DE S'ANCRER DÈS QUE LE PHARE ÉCLATE DE SES AMERS
DANS UNE MAGNITUDE QU'AVOISINENT LES LIMITROPHES

I et Tour du Planier

PAR JOUR DE VENT VIOLENT MENAÇANT À TEMPÉTUEUSES
INTERMITTENTES SUR LES BAROMÉTRIQUES BRUSQUEMENT
EFFONDRÉES QUI SE DÉROBENT AUX PRÉVISIBLES AINSI
CONCEVABLES DANS LES MOMENTANÉES AUX ABORDS D'UN
AFFAIBLISSEMENT THERMIQUE QUASI ARCTIQUE DONT LE
GRADIENT CONDENSE SEULEMENT LES VAPEURS EXHALÉES
PAR LES SEPTENTRIONALES À CRAINDRE PROCHAINEMENT
DANS LE COULOIR QUI ENGENDRE LE MAGISTRAL TOURNÉ
EN NŒUDS D'ACCALMIE PASSAGÈRE ATTÉNUÉE SOUS LES
DIVISIONS DU LOCH AU MILLE DES NAUTIQUES HISSÉES
JUSQU'AU DÉFERLEMENT MALGRÉ LE LEST À CHARGE DES
PORTÉES FRACASSANTES QUE LES BOURRASQUES ENFLENT
D'UN GALBE IMPÉTUEUX LIBÉRANT LEURS EMBRUNS AVEC
L'AGRESSIVE DES BRISES AUX SAUTES IMMINENTES QUI
S'ÉLONGENT EN RÉVOLUTION PARALLÈLE À LA CAMBRURE
PLANÉTAIRE RALENTISSANT DE CE FROTTEMENT ROTATIF
DONT LES PARAMÈTRES S'OPPOSENT ET QUE LE PÉNIBLE
GLISSEMENT HEURTE DÈS QU'IL S'AGIT D'ÉVALUER LES
RIDES AU GABARIT DES ISOBARES SUR L'ORDINAIRE DE
L'EMBELLIE D'OÙ S'ENTREPREND TELLE TRAVERSÉE PAR
UN APPAREILLAGE SANS CRAINTE DES PÉRILS EN DÉPIT
DES NAUFRAGES QUE L'AVARIE PROVOQUE AU MOUILLAGE
DE LAMES DANS UN RETOURNEMENT CONTRE LES ACCORES
À ANFRACTUOSITÉS FRAPPÉES SOUS LE CHOC DU RESSAC

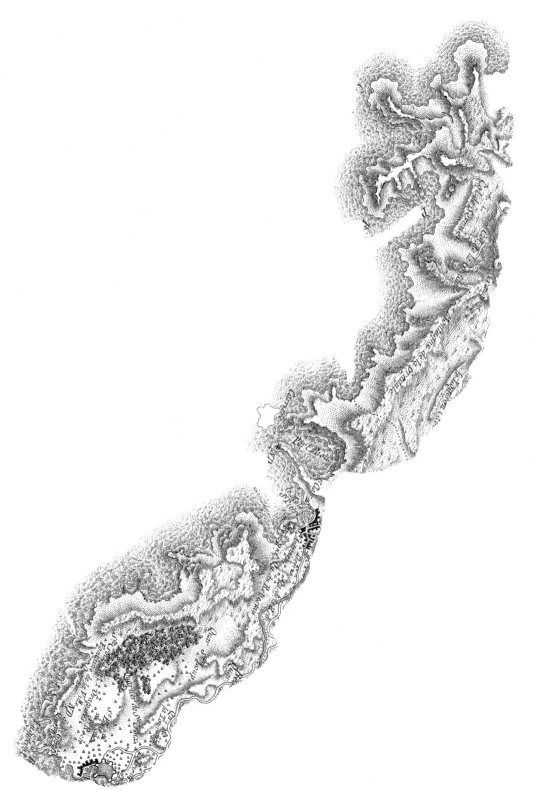

TRAÇANT LA LIGNE IMAGINAIRE ENTRE FLUX ET REFLUX
QUE L'ÉTALON COURBE EN SAILLIES LÉGALES CREUSÉES
AU LARGE DES HOULEUSES BOURSOUFLÉES À MESURE DES
CONJONCTIONS QUI RYTHMENT L'AMPLITUDE EXACTE DES
NIVEAUX ALORS QUE LA VISÉE INSTANTANÉE NÉCESSITE
UN AJUSTEMENT À ÉCHELLE RÉDUITE DES ÉCARTS QU'UN
SIGNAL FIXE D'APRÈS L'ÉLÉVATION APPROXIMATIVE DE
LA SURFACE HORIZONTALE EN DIFFÉRENTS POINTS DONT
LA MOYENNE ARBITRAIRE COMPENSE LA LIMITE VISIBLE
GRÂCE À UNE GRADUATION ABSOLUE RÉGIE DURABLEMENT
PAR LE MARÉGRAPHE QUI CONTRÔLE L'INCOMMENSURABLE
ET ENREGISTRE TROUBLÉ SES VARIATIONS MATÉRIELLES
SANS POUVOIR INFLUER SUR UNE LOGIQUE QUI PROCÈDE
AVANT TOUT DE L'ATTRAIT POUR L'IMAGE CODIFIÉE DE
LA REPRÉSENTATION IGNORANT AINSI LA TRÈS FRAGILE
SENSATION D'ÉQUILIBRE ENTRE L'AU-DESSUS ET L'AU-
DESSOUS DONT LE DÉCOMPTE REND ENCORE PERCEPTIBLE
L'UNITÉ DE L'ABSENCE QUI SE RÉVÈLE SOURNOISEMENT
ATTISANT LA PEUR DU VIDE PAR SA GRANDEUR INFINIE
ET GÉNÈRE UNE VRAIE TENSION LORSQUE LA COHÉRENCE
D'UNE STABILITÉ RIGIDE SE ROMPT SOUS L'EFFET DES
DYNAMIQUES OSCILLATOIRES DONT LE COEFFICIENT EST
PROPORTIONNEL À L'ATTRACTION RÉELLE POUR CET AXE
VAIN QU'EXERCE LA DIMENSION CONSIDÉRABLE DU ZÉRO

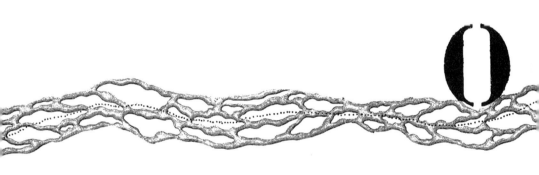

O

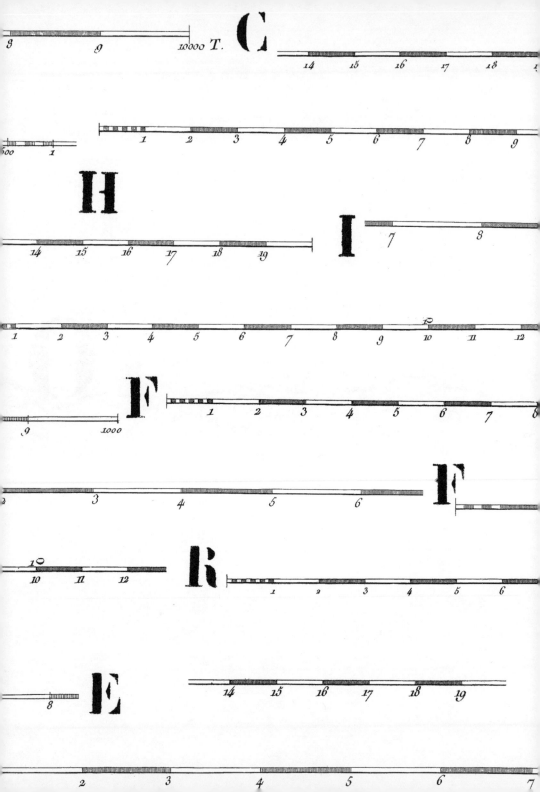

AU SERVICE DU CHIFFRE QUI BROUILLE AUSSI PAR SES
ENTRELACEMENTS LE SIGNE CLAIR DES FRÉQUENCES QUE
LES VOYELLES ENCORE TROP BUCCALES ASSOCIENT MAIS
EN LES TRANSPOSANT AUX INTELLIGIBLES QUI FONDENT
QUANT À ELLES LES VARIANTES D'UN TEXTE NUMÉRIQUE
DANS LEQUEL S'ALIGNENT LES SÉRIES EN COLONNES ET
OÙ LES LIGATURES PRENNENT L'APPARENCE DE LACUNES
PAR LES ARTIFICES DES CONVENTIONNELLES ALORS QUE
LE MESSAGE SE TRANSFORME DANS LES MARGES DU CODE
RÉDUIT À LA DISPROPORTION DE PLAUSIBLES ÉNONCÉES
EN COMBINAISONS ALPHABÉTIQUES QU'IL FAUT SURTOUT
SUBSTITUER LES UNES AUX AUTRES AVANT DE RÉÉCRIRE
AUX EMPLACEMENTS MARQUÉS PAR CERTAINES CLEFS LES
CONFIDENTIELLES ABRÉGÉES À L'INITIALE DU NOM QUE
LES RECOUPEMENTS FASTIDIEUX TRAHISSENT AU RISQUE
DE SE CONFONDRE AVEC CES INCOHÉRENTES ASSEMBLANT
PAR RUSE DES SÉQUENCES ERRONÉES DONT LE DÉCOMPTE
HÉSITANT JUSTIFIE LA TENEUR TRÈS EXACTE DES MOTS
DÉLICATS À AUTHENTIFIER AFIN DE NE PAS DIVULGUER
LE CRYPTOGRAMME EN PARODIE DE CALCUL ÉBAUCHÉE AU
HASARD DE DÉPÊCHES SANS LETTRE TRANSMISES PAR LE
DÉCHIFFREUR TOUT EN MASQUANT LES CORRESPONDANCES
PERMUTÉES ET SECRÈTES D'UNE ÉCRITURE STRATÉGIQUE
DISSIMULÉE DANS L'OUVRAGE ISOLÉ DU FOR INTÉRIEUR

CE BASTION À L'ANGLE MORT OÙ LA PAGE RESTÉE SOUS
SCELLÉS S'ENFERRE DANS L'IMPRESSION DE FAUTES EN
ESCORTE QUE L'OMISSION GUETTE À SON TOUR SANS LE
SIGNAL DU FANAL À LA PREMIÈRE ALERTE INSENSÉE DE
CET ARSENAL DE L'ESPRIT EN POSTE DÈS QUE LA NUIT
VERROUILLE SES REMPARTS AMÉNAGÉS AUX CRÉNEAUX DE
L'ENCEINTE ATTENTIVE BORNÉE PAR LES RONDES D'UNE
INVESTIGATION ÉVIDANT TOUS LES TRAITS EN RENFORT
DES APPUIS DÉCOCHÉS DANS UN RAYON RECTILIGNE QUE
LA FLÈCHE POINTE EN GRAPHIQUES AUX LINÉAMENTS DE
CONTOURS SYLLABIQUES PERCÉS DE MEURTRIÈRES SITÔT
ÉTABLIE LA COUPURE DANS L'ÉPAISSEUR DE LA VEILLE
QUI DÉFEND UN ACCÈS À CES VITALES FLANQUÉES D'UN
RUDE PROTOCOLE SUIVANT LEQUEL LES REPLIS ENGAGÉS
VERS LES POSITIONS CENTRALES DES FORMULES ORALES
SÉQUESTRÉES DANS LES FORTIFICATIONS DE LA PAROLE
DÉTIENNENT LES INEXPRIMABLES SOUVENT REBELLES AU
SUJET QUI S'INSURGE ET TENTE BIEN DE SE PROTÉGER
CONTRE L'ÉCOUTE CACHÉE AU SEUIL DE DÉTECTION DES
DANGERS IDENTIFIÉS SUR LE QUI-VIVE AVEC TOUS LES
MOBILES D'UN FAUX INTERROGATOIRE CONTENU DANS LE
RECUEIL DE PREUVES NOTÉES À SEULE FIN DE DÉPOSER
AU RECTO L'EMPREINTE DES FAITS D'ÉCRITS OBSERVÉS
PAR LA VIGIE QUI SUR LA COLLINE MONTE À LA GARDE

PRISE DES PERSPECTIVES PLONGEANTES OÙ FUIENT LES
IMAGINABLES À PERTE D'ACUITÉ SITÔT QUE L'ŒIL ET
SES ANNEXES PARCOURENT LE QUADRILLAGE TÉMOIN DES
COÏNCIDENCES EN CHAÎNE DONT L'ARPENTAGE DONNE LA
LÉGENDE AFIN DE LOCALISER LES ÉQUIDISTANCES SOUS
LES HACHURES DES RÉDUCTIONS À L'INTERSECTION DES
SEGMENTS BITUMÉS QUI SE RACCORDENT AUX TRAVERSES
EN RACCOURCIS SOLIDAIRES DES EMMARCHEMENTS POSÉS
PAR PALIERS À DOUBLE VOLÉE DONT LA RAMPE COURANT
AU CŒUR DES GIRATOIRES SOULIGNE LE PARTAGE DOSÉ
DES DEGRÉS À FRANCHIR JUSQU'À L'ALLÉE VENUE D'UN
ENTOUR PLUS ENCOMBRÉ AVEC SES CHAUSSÉES SATURÉES
D'URBANISATION ÉCRASANTE OÙ L'ERRANCE TRAQUÉE EN
SES IMPASSES LES PLUS INTIMES MAINTIENT EN GRAND
RENFERMEMENT LES RAGEUSES MURÉES PAR PANS QUI SE
LÉZARDENT AU PIGNON QUAND LE CADRAGE DES DROITES
IMPOSE SES VISUELLES CAVALIÈRES QUI SE REPORTENT
SYMÉTRIQUEMENT COMME LES OPTIQUES D'UNE ILLUSION
RÉTICULAIRE PROJETÉE SUR LE LABYRINTHE TRAMÉ QUI
PLANTE SES JALONS EN AGGLOMÉRATION D'UNE TEXTURE
ÉCHUE AUX CADASTRALES FIGURÉES MALGRÉ LE FONCIER
DES SOLIDES AGRAIRES DONT IL FAUT REPÉRER À MAIN
LEVÉE LES PARCELLAIRES AVANT D'ESQUISSER DANS UN
PLAN PLUS RAPPROCHÉ L'ÉPURE D'UNE VILLE SANS NOM

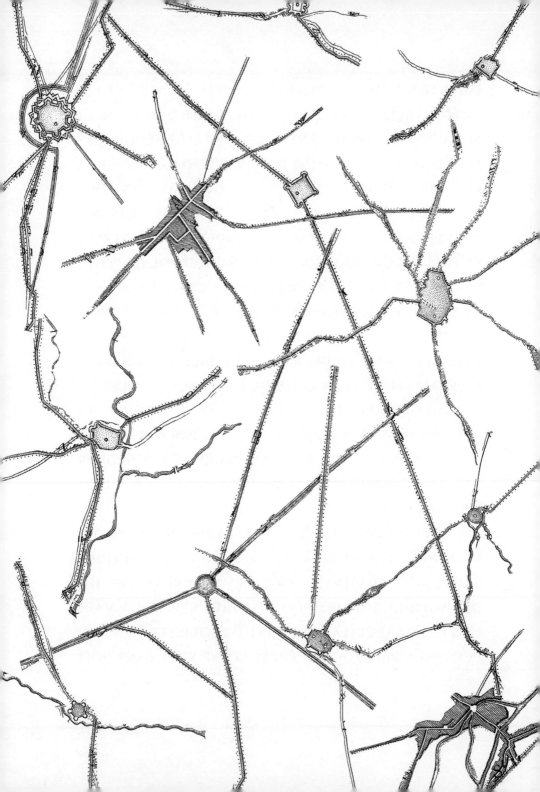

TOUJOURS LATENTE EN SON INDÉPENDANCE QUI EMPIÈTE
À LA DÉMESURE DES EXCÈS SUR LES IMPÉRIEUSES D'OÙ
LES TYRANNIQUES SE DÉCHAÎNENT CONTRE CES OUTRÉES
PEU DOCILES EN SOMME LORSQUE D'ABUSIVES CHÂTIÉES
SONT ASTREINTES À UNE REPENTANCE DE MAUVAISE VIE
QUE LES FANATISMES ASSUJETTISSENT RÉDUISANT TOUT
LIEN À L'EFFET QUE CAUSE LA FAUTE BATTUE HORS SA
COULPE COMME L'AMÈRE EXPIATION DES CAPTIVES DONT
LE JOUG SECOUE LES INTOLÉRABLES QUI CONTRAIGNENT
AUX DÉSHONNEURS DES MŒURS ALORS QUE BRUTALEMENT
LES INDIGENTES EXPULSÉES DU REFUGE SE DÉLIENT DE
LA LANGUE EN VERNACULAIRES CHARNUES QUI CLAQUENT
AU PASSAGE DES INVECTIVES ET NARGUENT VIOLEMMENT
LES RÉPRESSIVES AFIN D'ÉCHAPPER À UN ÉTOUFFEMENT
DES PAPILLES SOUS LE BÂILLON DE L'EXPRESSION QUI
ACCABLE LE SENS EN ÉCHEC LORSQUE LA FOLIE DE CES
EXIGUËS SURMÈNE LES HYPERTROPHIÉES DÉTENUES DANS
UN CLOISONNEMENT RETORS DES PARLERS QUI EXCLUENT
À L'ÉTROIT DES PHRASÉS PRESSURANT LES PRONONCÉES
DE L'AUTRE PART ET EMPÊCHENT LES PROPOS ÉPANCHÉS
QUE LE DIRE MUSELÉ HÉSITE À RELÂCHER NÛMENT SAUF
QUAND À DEMI-MOT DE LEUR RÉVOLTE LES AFFRANCHIES
DES SYNTAXES S'INGÉNIENT DORÉNAVANT À TROUVER LÀ
À L'AVERS DES RATURES LES PLUS ULTIMES TOURNURES

À LA GLORIEUSE MÉMOIRE DES COMMÉMORATIVES GRAVES
EN LEURS SENSIBLES QUI EXPRIMENT LE SOUVENIR DES
RECULÉES D'UN TEMPS DERNIER DANS UNE CHRONOLOGIE
QUE L'INDÉTERMINATION CONSACRE AUX RÉVOLUS MOINS
PRÉCIS DANS LEURS CHANGEMENTS ET PLUS PROPICES À
RAVIVER LES ÉPHÉMÉRIDES QUI FLANCHENT À FORCE DE
SE REMÉMORER LES OUBLIEUX DANS UN RAPPEL INSCRIT
AU FRONTON DES CORNICHES EN ENCORBELLEMENT AINSI
QU'AU REVERS DES EX-VOTO CONCIS ENCORE ACCROCHÉS
AUX PHÉNOMÈNES PAR LA SOUVENANCE TENACE ET INDUE
PLEINE D'INCERTITUDES QUANT À L'AUTHENTICITÉ DES
FABULEUX VESTIGES QUE LES RÉTINIENNES ASSIMILENT
PAR ANALOGIE AUX RÉMINISCENCES D'UN PASSÉ ÉTEINT
QUI NE PERDURE DANS LES MENTALES QU'À L'AIDE DES
RECONNAISSANTES ARCHIVÉES SELON DES CONCORDANCES
PEU OBJECTIVES SUR LES MONUMENTAUX ANTÉRIEURS AU
CONTINUEL DES ANNALES PARFOIS AMNÉSIQUES QUE LES
TOURNANTS D'HISTORIQUES À PEINE PÉRIMÉS OMETTENT
AU FUR ET À MESURE DE LEURS EXCAVATIONS ANTIQUES
EN DÉBLAI DE FOUILLES QUI RAPPORTENT D'OBSOLÈTES
VÉCUS DIGNES DU RESSOUVENIR SANS RÉPIT QUI HANTE
LA MNÉMONIQUE OPPRESSANTE ALORS QUE LE NARRATEUR
INTRUS EXACERBE SES PERCEPTIVES OCCUPÉ À SCRUTER
DU CIEL OUVERT LA PERPÉTUITÉ D'UN SUD IMMÉMORIAL

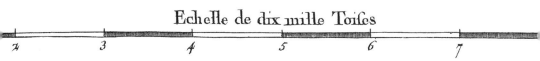

Echelle de dix mille Toises

2   3   4   5   6   7

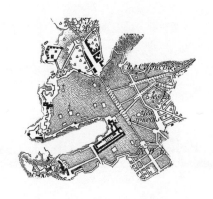

MARSEILLE

Légende

Horizon du sol : accumulation d'éléments dans une couche géologique. Ainsi ce recueil, qui s'invente par apports successifs, mêlant des éléments très divers :

Le calibre des textes : 24 lignes de 48 signes, il découle du nombre de lettres de l'alphabet provençal.

Le matériau des collages : il provient de la carte de Cassini (XVIIIᵉᵐᵉ siècle), si proche de l'écriture dans son usage du trait. L'image est un poème.

La ville littorale : elle se situe au point de contact entre la lithosphère, l'atmosphère et l'hydrosphère.

Le panorama : champ visuel / champ sémantique.

La transgression : c'est la mer qui recouvre le "continent perdu", continent sud-provençal dont les géologues font l'hypothèse. Transgression dans le langage.

Le marégraphe : situé sur la Corniche, il déterminait le nivellement général de la France. Muré depuis peu.

Le service du chiffre : chargé de transmettre les messages secrets à partir du Fort Saint-Nicolas.

La colline de la Garde : ancien emplacement de la vigie.

Le magistral : vent maître, mistral en provençal.

Les noms de lieu : la barrière du coupe-feu, l'île Plane, l'impasse des Intimes, la rue des Honneurs (anc. Déshonneur), le Refuge…

Les inscriptions : relevées sur les monuments, les plaques : par jour de vent violent… (escalier mécanique du Centre Bourse) ; le monument du grand renfermement (Vieille Charité) ; à la glorieuse mémoire… (rue Pierre Dessemond).

Les allusions historiques : "la ville sans nom" ; "l'indépendance de la cité toujours latente".

Il a été tiré de cet ouvrage, composé par (sic)
et imprimé par l'Imprimerie Saint-Lambert à Marseille,
huit cent cinquante exemplaires :

cinquante exemplaires sur vélin de Lana
numérotés de 1 à 50,

huit cents exemplaires sur Centaure Ivoire,

et quelques exemplaires hors commerce,
constituant l'édition originale de :

LES HORIZONS DU SOL

trente deuxième livre de la collection
'''Le Refuge'''
achevé d'imprimer le 22 janvier 1999

Dépôt légal : 01/1999 - Éditeur : 1032
ISBN : 2-909097-31-5

About the Author

The author of more than two dozen books of poetry and translations from the Chinese, Michèle Métail has been broadcasting her work in so-called *Publications orales* since 1973, in particular "Poème infini (compléments de noms)," which is a single long modulation through a variety of languages and dialects. In the author's view, the projection of words into space is "the ultimate stage of writing," the affirmation of presence within language. Characterized by a rhythmical and musical approach to the text, and sometimes accompanied by slideshows, musicians, or taped sound, oral publications can take anything from ten minutes up to several hours. The exploration of the limits of meaning, the creation of semantic halos, and the frequently jagged syntax attempt to render the slight fuzziness of perception as it captures reality. Although Métail's writing is nourished by contact with the world and by travel, encounters and meetings between various modes of expression are just as indispensable to her. Together with composer Louis Roquin, she is the cofounder of Les arts contigus, an association which likes to explore genre transgression. In 2019, she was the recipient of the Bernard Heidseick Award of Honor. *Les horizons du sol* resulted from a three-month residency at cipM, centre international de poesie Marseille, in 1998; it will be her first book of poetry to be published in English.

About the Translator

Marcella Durand's books of poetry include *The Prospect* (Delete Press, 2019), *Rays of the Shadow* (Tent Editions, 2017), *Le Jardin de M.* (The Garden of M.), with French translations by Olivier Brossard (joca seria, 2016), *Deep Eco Pré*, a collaboration with Tina Darragh, *AREA*, and *Traffic & Weather*, written during a residency at the Lower Manhattan Cultural Council. She lives in the Lower East Side in New York City with her husband and son, and is working on a new manuscript involving septentrionals and constellations.